Amazing Changing 1921 S
VAM 1B
Thorn Head Morgan Dollar

by

Leroy C. Van Allen

Revised January 2009

Thorn Gouge and Cap Gouge

Die Gouge IB

Die Gouges Y and Cap

Published by

Rare Coin Investments (RCI)
P.O. Box C
Ironia, NJ 07845

Copyright © 2025 by Michael S. Fey, Ph.D.

Authors: Leroy C. Van Allen
Edited by: Michael S. Fey, Ph.D.

ISBN-13 number: 979-8-9919648-2-1

Printed in the United States

TABLE OF CONTENTS

LIST OF FIGURES

LIST OF CHARTS

INTRODUCTION

The 1921 S VAM 1B Morgan dollar is known as the **"Thorn Head"** die variety because one of it's die states shows a prominent spike of a die gouge protruding from the top of the Phrygian cap of the Liberty head as shown in Figure 1. But that is only a part of the *amazing* life of the **obverse** die of this 1921 S Morgan VAM 1B, Thorn Head sub-variety of the normal die 1. At some point during this obverse die's early lifetime, it first received two large die gouges at the top and back of the Phrygian cap plus two small die gouges near UN of UNUM. But that was just the beginning of a series of damages and subsequent polishing repairs on this obverse die at the San Francisco Mint. These later damages of the die added *six* more deep and large die gouges in the fields, *two* more in the denticles and lastly, *one* thru Y of LIBERTY. There are currently known **nine distinct die gouge states** of this obverse die with various numbers and strengths of the *thirteen* die gouges. And to cap it off, the **reverse** die also shows *two* significant die gouges with the last three obverse die gouge states!

These nine sequences of die damage and repair polishing is, by far, the *most extensive* and *spectacular* of any Morgan dollar variety! The 1921 S VAM 1B is not listed as either a Top 100 or Hot 50 die variety, a major oversight for collectors, but perhaps because of it's rarity. However, it has been known since reported in 1978 and is listed and pictured as VAM 1B with the thorn-like die gouge in the so-called VAM book, *Comprehensive Catalog and Encyclopedia of Morgan and Peace Dollars*, 3rd ed. 1992 and 4th ed. 1998, by Leroy C. Van Allen & A. George Mallis.

Each die state that had die gouges added or removed is given a sub-sub-variety **number**. Thus, the initial die state that had four die gouges added is designated VAM 1B1. The second die state that removed a die gouge at the back of the Phrygian cap is designated VAM 1B2. The third die state added the thorn-like die gouge from the right wheat leaf and is designated 1B3. This thorn-like gouge was mostly removed by polishing and is designated 1B3a since no new die gouges were added or completely removed. This same die designation procedure was carried out for the remaining die states.

The **five** **damaged** die states and subsequent **four** die **polishing** repairs are described and illustrated in this report. The **dates** when the various die states were first reported and **who** reported them is also pointed out. A separate section lists and illustrates the **key identifiers** for each die state. Another later section contains the **descriptive listings** of each die state. A final section contains all of the **photographs** for each die state variety.

Figure 1 1921 S VAM 1B3 Thorn Head

INCREDIBLE PROBLEMS WITH COINING PRESS AND DIES

The 1921 S VAM 1B Thorn Head die variety has been known since 1978 when a die state was first reported by Martin Field that had a thorn-like die gouge above the Phrygian cap. Additional die states were not reported until much later in 2002 thru 2008. Those reporting the new die states include John Baumgart, Michael Fey, Rob Joyce and Brian Raines. At this current point in time it is thought that most, if not all, of the die states of this **amazing** obverse die variety have been found and reported. So the complete sequences of events for this VAM 1B Thorn Head die variety can finally be told.

It must have been very *frustrating* for the mint worker who operated the coining press at the San Francisco Mint for this pair of dies. A rather obvious large horizontal die gouge **suddenly** appeared on the obverse **Phrygian cap near the fold** as shown in Figure 2 and one at the **back of the cap** in the field as shown in Figure 3. A small die gouge is also in the field next to the **rear of the cap fold** as shown in Figure 4 and a small one in the **denticles above N** in UNUM, also shown in Figure 4. The obverse die was then likely removed from the coining press and the gouge in the field at the cap back near UM of UNUM was polished away. The gouge in the cap **recesses** could not be removed by the flat polishing wheel because it was in the recesses below the fields of the die. Once back in the coining press, the die was damaged again with a long **thorn-like gouge** in the field to the right of the **right wheat leaf** as shown in Figure 5. This die state was the initial one reported in 1978 and resulted in the moniker **"Thorn Head"** for this die variety.

The mint worker dutifully removed the die and polished most of this thorn die gouge away. Once back in the coining press, the die was subsequently damaged again with a **long gouge thru IB** of PLURIBUS as shown in Figure 6 and another **gouge thru NU** of UNUM as shown in Figure 7. The obverse die was polished again weakening the gouges at IB and NU and returned to service. Unfortunately the die was damaged again with new **gouges appearing above B** in PLURIBUS as shown in Figure 8, at the cap back **in the field at NU** as shown in Figure 9 and two visible gouges in the **denticles** at the **fourth left star** as shown in Figure 10 and one at the **second right star** as shown in Figure 11. Curiously, gouges also appeared on the **reverse die** between **E-D** of ONE DOLLAR as shown in Figure 12 and **below the eagle's left wing** as shown in Figure 13 which remained thru the subsequent die states.

Once again the obverse die was polished, but this time so extensively that most of the gouges in the fields were removed. The obverse die was put back into service but subsequently received a strong long **die gouge thru Y** in LIBERTY as shown in Figure 14. This is the **final** known die state for VAM 1B die variety. This final die gouge at Y was also in the recesses of the die and couldn't be polished out by a flat polishing wheel. At this point the mint worker apparently **gave up** on trying to repair the obverse die and it was retired after **five** separate episodes of receiving die **damage** of thirteen visible die gouges and **four** attempts at **polishing repairs** resulting in **nine** known die states! The reverse die was never polished to repair the two die gouges.

The poor mint worker really had a *bad day* with this thorn head die! The mint press must have then under gone repair at some point, either after the thorn head episodes or possibly after the separate obverse die of VAM 1A that has a die scratch at BU in PLURIBUS.

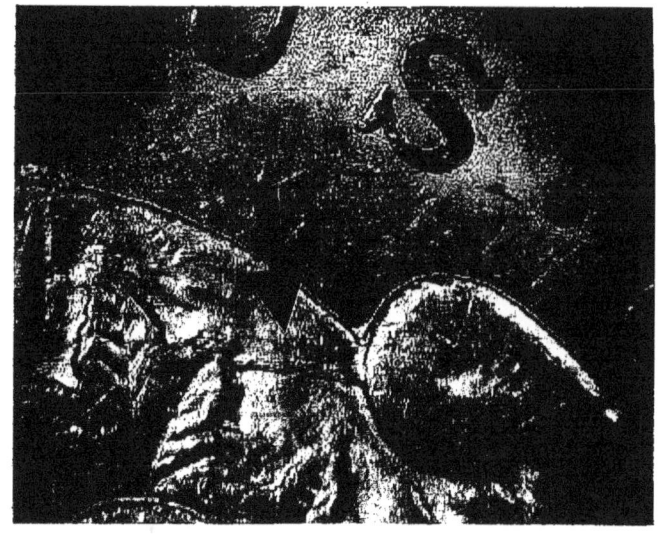

Figure 2 VAM 1B1 Die Gouge in Cap
1st Die State

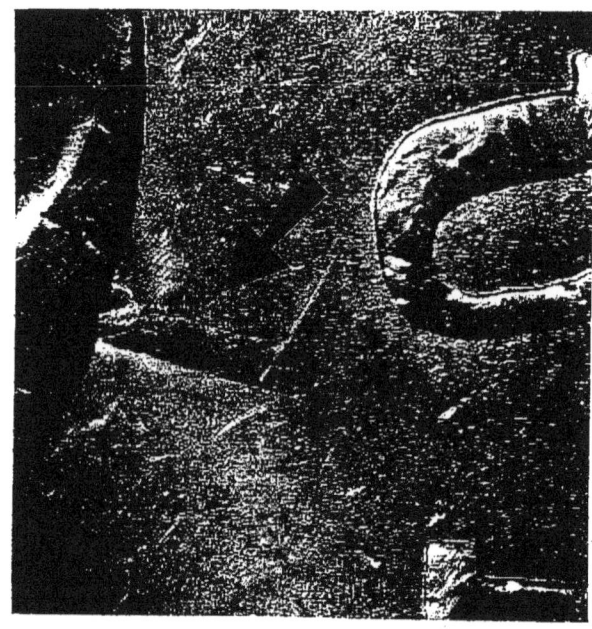

Figure 3 VAM 1B1 Die Gouge Cap Back
1st Die State

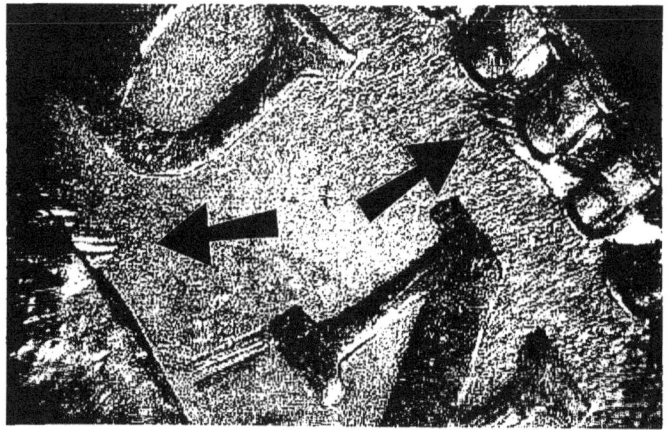

Figure 4 VAM 1B1 Die Gouges Cap Back & Above N
1st Die State

Figure 5 VAM 1B3 Thorn Head Die Gouge
3rd Die State

Figure 6 VAM 1B4 Die Gouge IB
5th Die State

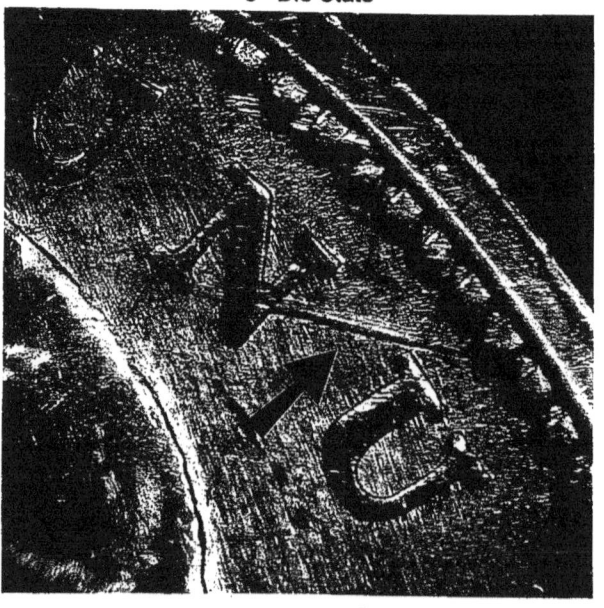

Figure 7 VAM 1B4 Die Gouge NU
5th Die State

-4-

Figure 8 VAM 1B5 Die Gouge IB
7th Die State

Figure 9 VAM 1B5 Die Gouge NU & Cap
7th Die State

Figure 10 VAM 1B5 Die Gouges
4th Left Star
7th Die State

Figure 11 VAM 1B5 Die Gouge 2nd Rt. Star
7th Die State

Figure 13 VAMs 1B5-7 Spike Eagle's Left Wing

Figure 14 VAM 1B7 Die Gouge Y & Cap
9th Die State

Figure 12 VAMs 1B5-7 Die Gouge ED on Reverse

CAUSES OF DIE GOUGES

The 1921 S VAM 1B obverse die experienced an almost *unbelievable* series of **die gouges** and **polishing**, the **most** on a Morgan dollar die!! Perhaps a faulty die polishing wheel caused these recurring deep die gouges. But a *flat die polishing wheel* would likely cause die gouges at **various** places in the die fields and with more **curvature** on the gouge lines. However, for the VAM 1B die gouges, were **straight** and primarily at the **upper right quadrant** of the obverse die. Also, the flat polishing wheel and wouldn't cause the deep gouges in the recesses of the Liberty head in the die.

A more plausible explanation is that the hardened **feed fingers** edges were somehow jammed upwards into the obverse hammer die as the feed fingers moved back and forth. The sharp feed finger edges would produce fairly straight die gouges in the same general location and area (In this case the top right cap and field.). The orientation of the dies in the coining press must have been with the dies about crosswise to the feed fingers operation direction to produce the straight gouges horizontally across the top right of the obverse. The feed fingers edges could have somehow been raised up into the Phrygian cap die cavity to produce the gouges there. Figure 15 shows a canceled 1884 Morgan obverse die with incuse design and recessed denticles.

The feed fingers consisted of two long flat steel strips that opened and closed and went in and out between the lower reverse die and upper obverse die of the coining press for the Morgan dollars. Feed fingers and the collar that surrounds the coins when being struck are shown in Figure 16 for equipment used in the 1970s for the dual die set-up of dimes. Figure 17 shows the feed fingers and upper dies in a coining press in the 1970s which would be similar to coining presses used to strike the 1921 S Morgan dollar. Figure 18 shows the No. 1 press for the Carson City Mint and Figure 19 shows a close-up of the feed finger tracks. The feed fingers perform two functions of laying the blank into the collar over the reverse die and pushing the newly struck coin off the lower reverse die when it has risen above the collar.

Figure 20 shows a diagram of the feed finger and die operation as coins are being struck in the coining press. First, the feed chutes drop the coin blank into the open feed fingers atop a flat surface. The feed fingers are two long arms which pivot together gripping the blank between the two semi-circular cutouts. Then the closed feed fingers advance between a raised upper die and a dropped lower die. As the feed fingers pivot apart, the blank drops down into the collar to rest on top of the lower die. The feed fingers then retract back out from between the dies. The upper and lower dies come together on the blank impressing the obverse and reverse designs and causing the metal to flow outwards against the collar. The upper die raises up first and then the lower die raises up slightly to push the coin up out of the collar. Then the closed feed fingers advance with a fresh blank **simultaneously** pushing the newly struck coin off the raised lower die into the ejection chute with the closed ends of the feed fingers. Thus, the closed feed fingers ends are **between the dies** each coining cycle when they push the struck coin off the reverse die and advance to drop the planchet into the collar.

It is possible with a faulty press mechanism that the feed fingers got out of sync with the die vertical movement, or somehow got struck by a die and was slightly bent enough to scrape the die, or got loose, or jumped out of their track, or the lower reverse die somehow pushed the feed fingers upwards into the obverse die. It is not known at this point exactly how the feed fingers edges could have damaged the dies, but likely a bent edge scrapped the obverse die. The reverse die also show some gouges with the later three obverse die gouge states. Perhaps the feed fingers edges somehow also damaged the reverse die. Thus, the obverse die kept receiving gouges between polishes until it was permanently removed from the coining press and the press mechanism was fixed.

Why the **beleaguered** coining press operator didn't have the press mechanism fixed after the first couple die gouges instead of pressing on and attempting to repair the die with polishing after each of four episodes of die damage, is a mystery. For collectors, the **1921 S VAM 1B Thorn Head** nine die gouge states presents a **unique**, **challenging** and **wonderful** collecting opportunity!!

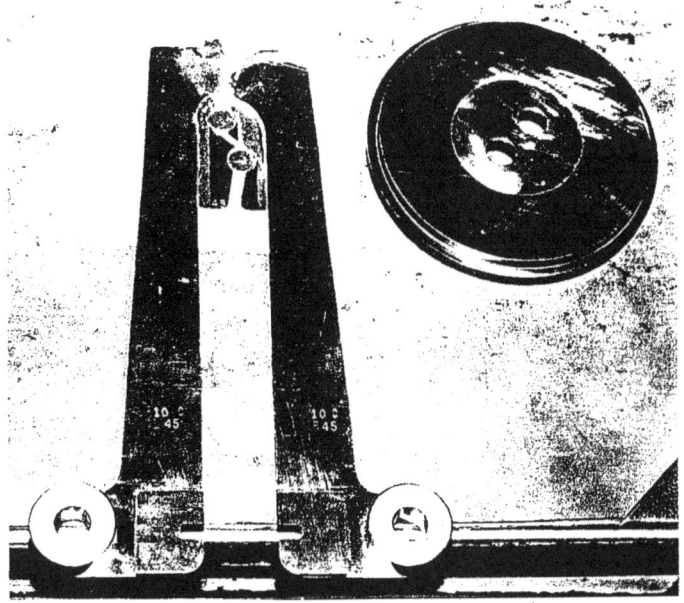

Figure 16 Feed Fingers and Collar, 1970s

Figure 17 Feed Fingers & Upper Dies in Press, 1970s

Figure 15 Canceled 1884 Morgan Obverse Die

Figure 18 No. 1 Press For Carson City Mint

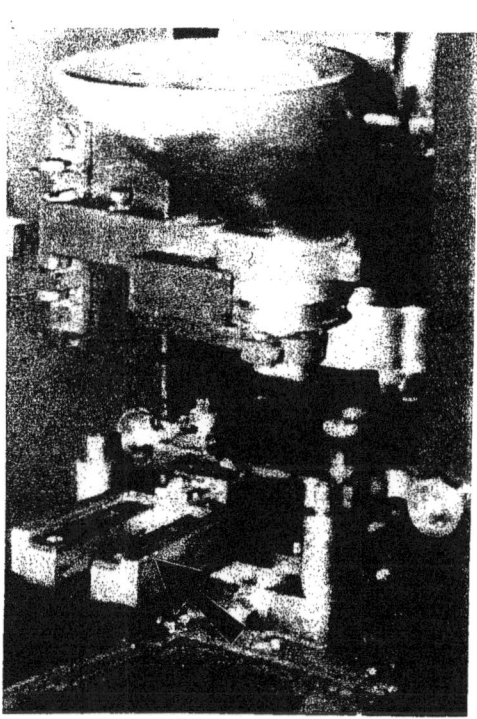

Figure 19 Carson City Press Feed Fingers Tracks

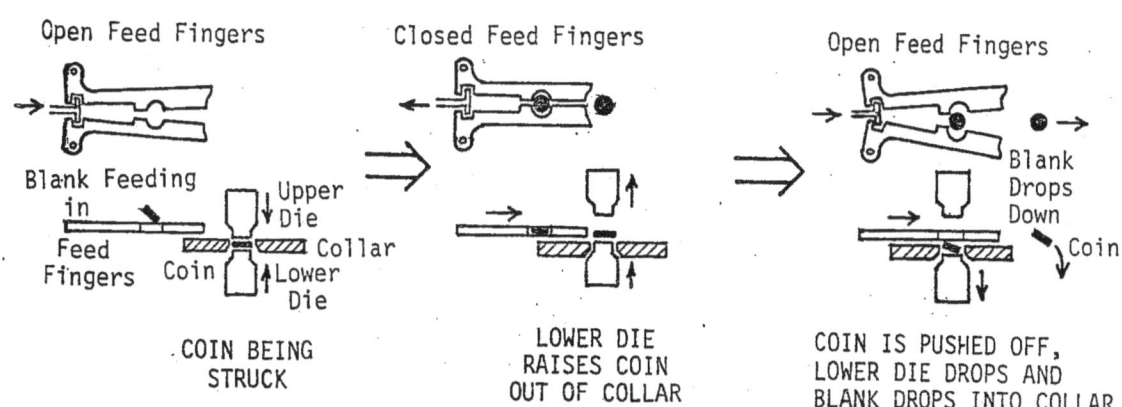

Figure 20 Feed Finger and Die Operation

REPORTING OF VARIOUS DIE GOUGE STATES

It should be noted that the **initial** die state with **no die gouges** can be identified by the unique fine **scribbling die scratches** at the eagle's right leg. These scratches were put there on most 1921 reverse dies by mint workman to fill in blank areas of the upper tail feathers caused by the basining and polishing of the dies. The scratches are shown in the last section of photographs of all the die states. The scribbling die scratches for the 1921 S VAM 1B was reported by Leroy Van Allen in October 2007.

The **first** of nine obverse die gouge states, die sub-sub-variety (or variety for short here) **1B1**, has four die gouges at the top of the Liberty head. A deep and long gouge band at the top of the Phrygian cap extends from the right of the top cotton leaf to the cap fold. This die gouge remains the same during subsequent die polishing because it was recessed in the cap die cavity and was not touched by the flat die polishing wheel. A wide thorn-like die gouge is in the field next to the cap and below the second U in UNUM. In addition, a short series of die gouge lines is in the field next to the rear of the cap field and a short die gouge is in the denticles above N in UNUM. This initial or first die gouge state doesn't show any polishing lines in the obverse fields. It was actually fifth to the last to be reported of the known die states and was reported in March 2003 by Rob Joyce.

The **second** die gouge state, die variety **1B2**, was the third to last one to be reported and was by John Baumgart in December 2003. The obverse die was heavily polished with polishing lines in the top right field and around the neck. This removed the thorn-like die gouge from the field next to the cap middle back. The die gouges in the cap, in the field behind the cap fold and in the denticles above N remained. No new die gouges were added.

The **third** die gouge state, die variety **1B3**, was the first one to be discovered and was reported by Martin Field in October 1978. It is pictured as VAM 1B in the so-called VAM book, *Comprehensive Catalog and Encyclopedia of Morgan and Peace Dollars,* 3rd ed. 1992 and 4th ed. 1998, by Leroy C. Van Allen and A. George Mallis. The obverse shows heavy polishing lines in the top right field of the second die state. The die gouges in the cap, in the field behind the cap fold and in the denticles above N remain. A *new* long thorn-like die gouge is added in the field to the right of the right wheat leaf above the Phrygian cap. Because this new prominent die gouge has the appearance of a sharp tapered thorn, this die gouge variety received the name **"Thorn Head"** back in 1978.

A polished version of the third die state was reported by John Baumgart in December 2008. Most of the thorn-like die gouge in the field to the right of the right wheat leaf was removed and part of the right wheat leaf. There remained faint lines of the gouge to the left and right of the wheat leaf. Other die gouges in the cap, field behind the cap fold and in the denticles above N also remained. Many polishing lines were added to the top field. Since no new gouges were added or old ones completely removed, this die state was given a **fourth** designation of die variety **1B3a**.

The description of the VAM 1B Thorn Head die gouge (die state 3) remained the same for almost 25 years until sharp-eyed Herb Zepke, in March of 2002, reported some added die gouges to what appeared to be a VAM 1B later die state. In this **fifth** die gouge state, die variety **1B4**, the thorn-like gouge in the field to the right of the right wheat leaf had mostly *disappeared* from die polishing of the VAM 1B3a die state. The ones in the cap die cavity to the right of the top cotton leaf, in the field behind the cap fold and in the denticles above N *remained* as in the 1B3a die state. Two *new* deep and long die gouges appeared in the top field between IB in LIBERTY and NU in UNUM.

In September 2003, Brian Raines reported that this fifth die state received further polishing which weakened the existing die gouges. No new die gouges were added. Since no die gouges were removed or added, it was given a **sixth** die state designation of die variety **1B4a**.

This discovery of polishing and addition of die gouges was astonishing enough, but the die gouge story was extended when Michael Fey reported in October 2002 what was thought to be a VAM 1B but with a thorn-like die gouge at the back of the cap instead of the top and another 1921 S with the original die gouge in the cap but none in the fields. It turns out that Fey's two coins were the seventh and eighth states of the die gouges and polishing. The **seventh** die gouge state, die variety **1B5**, still showed faint remains of the original thorn-like die gouge on either side of the top right wheat leaf. The long die gouge band in the cap and the short die gouge in denticles above N remained. The gouges thru IB and NU had now been polished so they were *weak* but still visible with fine polishing lines around them. But incredibly, a *new* long and deep die gouge had been added above the B and a *new* *thorn-like* wide and deep die gouge now appeared at the back of the cap between NU. An added tenth short die gouge appeared from the denticles into the field above the fourth left star, an eleventh in the denticles next to the fourth left star and a twelfth in the denticles next to the second right star.

Fey's other 1921 S showed the **eighth** and next to last die gouge state, die variety **1B6**, where most of the die gouges in the fields had been *removed* with extensive polishing lines in the fields and some shallow lettering and denticles. *Tiny remains* of the field die gouges still showed around the right wheat leaf, thru the top loop of B and a couple fine lines at the cap back. The long die gouge band in the cap to the right of the top cotton leaf still *remained* as do the gouges in the denticles above N, in denticles next to the second right star and in the denticles near the fourth left star.

Finally, in April 2004, Michael Fey again reported another die state, the **ninth** one, die variety **1B7,** of this **fantastic** 1921 S obverse die. The obverse and reverse dies remained the same as die state 6 except the obverse die received a thirteenth die gouge. It shows as a broad bar from the lower left of the Y in LIBERTY up thru the top of Y to the left side of the upper cotton leaf. Surely the San Francisco Mint *gave up* using this obverse die at that point since there was no way to remove this new gouge in the recesses of the Liberty head hair and cap.

To add to this *incredible* story, the **reverse** die paired with the seventh, eighth and ninth obverse die gouge states shows an added thin die gouge between E and D below the wreath bow and a short vertical spike below the eagle's left wing. These reverse die gouges don't appear with the first through sixth obverse die gouge states even though the same reverse die was used. They were reported by Michael Fey in October 2002 when he reported the seventh and eighth obverse die states.

At this time, die gouge state VAM 1B7 is the rarest and 1B1, 1B3 & 1B3a are the next rarest. The remaining die states are about equally scarce and difficult to find. The ninth and last die gouge state, 1B7, likely was immediately retired from service after the final die gouge in the recesses of the Liberty head. Also, it is not as obvious to spot because the one remaining strong die gouge is in the cap and the other gouge is fairly well hidden across the Y in LIBERTY. There may still be more die gouge states to be discovered between the various polishes this die received.

The following is a summary suggested by John Baumgart in December 2008 of the known sequences of die damage and repair polishing for th 1921 S VAM 1B Thorn Head die variety:

SUMMARY OF 1921 S VAM 1B THORN HEAD DIE STATES

Die State	Sequence	Changes to Obverse Die
1B1	Die damage	cap gouge, 3 gouges in field cap back
1B2	Die polish	removed gouge lower cap back
1B3	Die damage	gouge added right of wheat leaf (Thorn-like)
1B3a	Die polish	weakened gouge at wheat leaf
1B4	Die damage	gouges added a IB & NU
1B4a	Die polish	weakened gouges at IB & NU
1B5	Die damage	gouges added above B, cap back at NU & 3 at stars
		Reverse gouges added at E-D & below wing
1B6	Die polish	removed most of gouges in fields
1B7	Die damage	gouge added thru Y in LIBERTY
		Mint gave up using dies at this point

KEY IDENTIFIERS

The following are the key identifiers and photographs for each of the 1921 S VAM 1B Thorn Head die gouge states. Note that **all die states** have the horizontal die **gouge in the Phrygian cap** in front of the cap fold. Complete descriptions of each die variety state are provided in the later section, 1921 S VAM 1B Thorn Head Die States Descriptive Listings. Detailed close-up photographs of each die variety state are provided in the last section, Photographs of 1921 S VAM 1B Die States.

1B1   **Gouge back of Phrygian cap** in field underneath and **to right** second U in UNUM.

1B2   **No gouge** back of cap in field and **right wheat leaf full** and not polished.

1B3   **Full thorn-like gouge** from **right wheat leaf** with no polishing (only on this die state).

1B3a   **Thorn-like gouge in field removed** and part of right wheat leaf. Faint lines remain in right wheat leaf and stalk. **No die gouges** at IB, above B or at 4th left star and 2nd right star.
(Not to be confused with 1B6 which has faint line thru B, gouges at stars, and gouges on reverse at E-D and below wing.)

1B4   **Gouges added at IB & NU.**

1B4a   Polished and **weakened gouges at IB & NU.**

1B5   **Gouges added above B,** back of cap in field underneath and **to left** second U in UNUM and at 4th left star and 2nd right star.

1B6   **Polished fields** with **faint lines** thru **right wheat leaf and B.** Faint gouges at 4th left star and 2nd right star. Gouge at E-D on reverse and below eagle's left wing.
(Not to be confused with 1B3a which doesn't have lines thru B, gouges at 4th left star and 2nd right star or reverse gouges at E-D and below wing on reverse.)

1B7   **Gouge thru Y** in LIBERTY.

1B1
(1st Die State)

VAM 1B1 Die Gouge Cap Back

1B2
(2nd Die State)

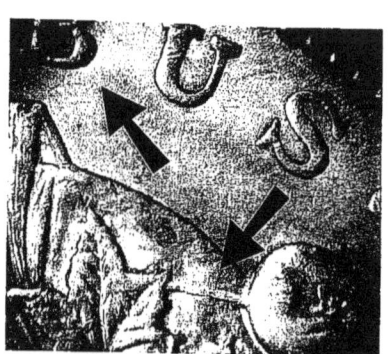

VAM 1B2 Die Gouge Cap
Full Rt. Wheat Leaf

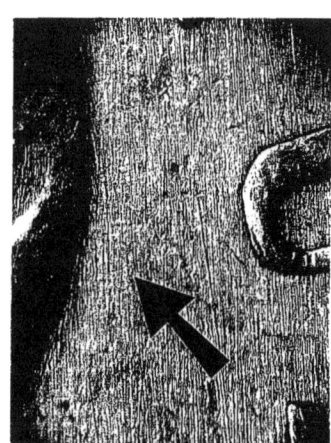

VAM 1B2 Polished Cap Back

1B3
(3rd Die State)

VAM 1B3 Thorn-Like Die Gouge
at Rt. Wheat Leaf

1B3a
(4th Die State)

VAM 1B3a Polished Thorn-Like
Die Gouge. No Lines in B

1B4
(5th Die State)

VAM 1B4 Die Gouge IB

1B4a
(6th Die State)

VAM 1B4a Polished Die Gouge IB

1B5
(7th Die State)

VAM 1B5 Die Gouge Above B

VAM 1B5 Die Gouge NU and Cap

1B6
(8th Die State)

VAM 1B6 Polished Die Gouges B

VAM 1B6 Die Gouge ED on Reverse

1B6
(Cont'd)

VAM 1B6 Polished Gouges 4th Left Star

VAM 1B6 Polished Die Gouge 2nd Rt. Star

1B7
(9th Die State)

VAM 1B7 Die Gouge Y

1921 S VAM 1B THORN HEAD DIE STATES DESCRIPTIVE LISTINGS

The initial die state without any die gouges is designated VAM 1B. It can be identified by the unique fine die scratches, or scribbles, at the eagle's right leg. The scribbles were scratched on the die before it was put into service in the coining press. These scribbles were a half-hearted attempt by the mint employees to fill in the flat blank area inside the eagle's leg that had parts of the upper tail feathers removed by the initial basining and polishing of the die.

Because of the large and very visible nature of the obverse die gouges, the various major die states showing them either added or removed, have been designated as die gouge sub-sub-varieties 1 thru 7 of the basic VAM 1B Thorn Head die sub-variety. Further, a couple cases of die polishing states that weakened the die gouges but did not have any die gouges added or removed are designated with a sub letter "a" for 1B3a and 1B4a. New die gouge damage or die polishing on the obverse die are referred to as die states with 9 currently known.

The descriptions of VAM 1B die states are as follows:

1921 S

1B(revised) IV 1 • D²a (Thorn Head Die Gouge, Scribbling Die Scratches #17) (189) I-3 R-6

Obverse IV 1– Slightly tripled right and some left stars.

Reverse D²a– Initial die state without die gouges. Various die states of die gouges listed as sub-varieties. Fine die scratches in various directions on over polished tail feathers around eagle's right leg, between eagle's left wing and body and in middle of eagle's left wing. *Die marker–* Single diagonal vee shaped polishing line on left side of lower outside feather in eagle's left wing.

1B1   IV 1 • D²a (Thorn Head Die Gouge, Die State 1)   (189)   I-5   R-6

Obverse IV 1– First die gouge state with four die gouges at top of Liberty head. A long die gouge band extends from right side of top left cotton leaf to left side of Phrygian cap fold. This long die gouge remains in all subsequent die states because it is recessed in a die cavity. A short series of die gouge lines is at back of cap fold in edge of field. A wide thorn-like die gouge is in field next to cap below second U in UNUM plus a short die gouge in denticles above N in UNUM. No evidence of die polishing.

1B2   IV 1 • D²a (Thorn Head Die Gouge, Die State 2)   (189)   I-5   R-6

Obverse IV 1– Second die gouge state with polished die removing thorn-like die gouge from field next to cap middle back. Die gouges in cap, in field behind cap field and in denticles above N remain. Extensive die polishing lines in top right field and some around neck.

1B3(revised) IV 1 • D²a (Thorn Head Die Gouge, Die State 3)   (189)   I-5   R-6

Obverse IV 1– Third die gouge state with polished die. Die gouges in cap, in field behind cap fold and in denticles above N remain. A long diagonal thorn-like die gouge is added in field to right of right wheat leaf above Phrygian cap. Polishing lines in top right field.

1B3a   IV 1 • D²a (Thorn Head Die Gouge, Die State 4)   (189)   I-5   R-7

Obverse IV 1– Polished version of die state 3 removing most of thorn-like die gouge in field to right of right wheat leaf and part of right wheat leaf, but leaving faint lines to left and right of wheat leaf. Die gouges in cap, in field behind cap fold and in denticles above N remain. Added more polishing lines in top field. No new gouges added or old ones removed.

1B4(revised) IV 1 • D²a (Thorn Head Die Gouge, Die State 5)   (189)   I-5   R-6

Obverse IV 1– Fifth die gouge state with prominent die gouge added between IB and diagonal die gouge added between NU in UNUM.

1B4a   IV 1• D²a (Thorn Head Die Gouges, Die State 6)   (189)   I-5   R-7

Obverse IV 1– Slightly polished version of die state 5 with weaker die gouges between IB and diagonal die gouge between NU and polishing lines evident around these gouges. No new gouges added or old ones removed.

1B5(revised) **IV 1 • D²a (Thorn Head Die Gouge, Die State 7)**   **(189)**   **I-5**   **R-6**

    Obverse IV 1– Seventh die gouge state with polished die removing die gouge in field behind cap fold and weakening die gouges between IB and NU. Die gouges in cap, in denticles above N and lines in wheat leaf remain. Added a long die gouge above B, a wide thorn-like die gouge in field at back of cap between NU, a short die gouge from denticles into field above fourth left star, one in denticles next to fourth left star and one in denticles below second right star. Clashed die but no clashed letters visible.

    Reverse D²a– Added thin die gouge between E and D below wreath bow and short vertical spike below eagle's left wing edge and tiny die scratch at top edge of top arrow head.

1B6(revised) **IV 1 • D²a (Thorn Head Die Gouge, Die State 8)**   **(189)**   **I-5**   **R-6**

    Obverse IV 1– Eighth die gouge state with die extensively polished removing most of die gouges in fields. Die gouges in cap, in denticles above N and in denticles below second right star remain. Faint die gouge remains to right and left of right wheat leaf, in top loop of B, back of cap between NU and in denticles near fourth left star. Later die state shows faint die clash line at neck.

    Reverse D²a– Die gouge between E and D and spike below eagle's left wing edge remain. Later die state shows vertical die clash line below In.

1B7   **IV 1 • D²a (Thorn Head Die Gouge, Die State 9)**   **(189)**   **I-5**   **R-7**

    Obverse IV 1– Nineth die gouge state that is same as die state 6 except a new long and wide die gouge was added thru Y in LIBERTY up to left side of top cotton leaf.

    Reverse D²a– Same die gouge between E & D and spike below eagle's left wing edge as in die states 5 & 6.

VAM 1B (No gouges)

VAM 1B Scribbling Die Scratches

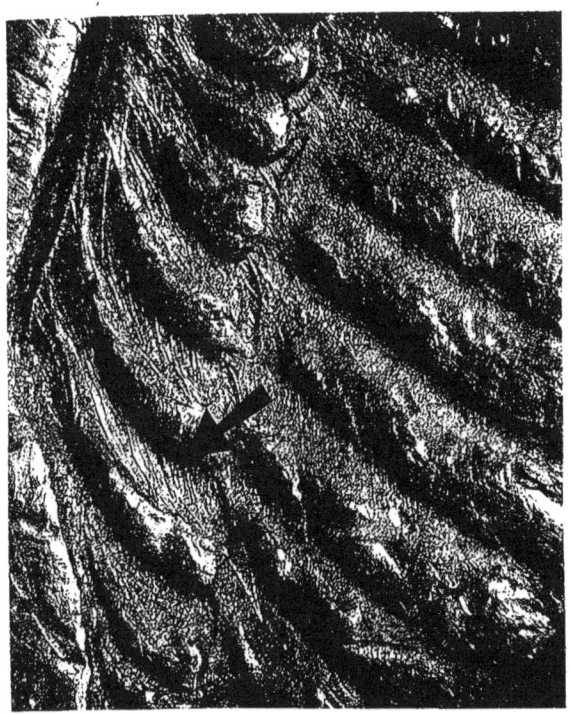

VAM 1B Scribbling Wing-Body

VAM 1B Polishing Vee Line

VAM 1B Scribbling Wing Middle

VAM 1B Doubled & Tripled Stars

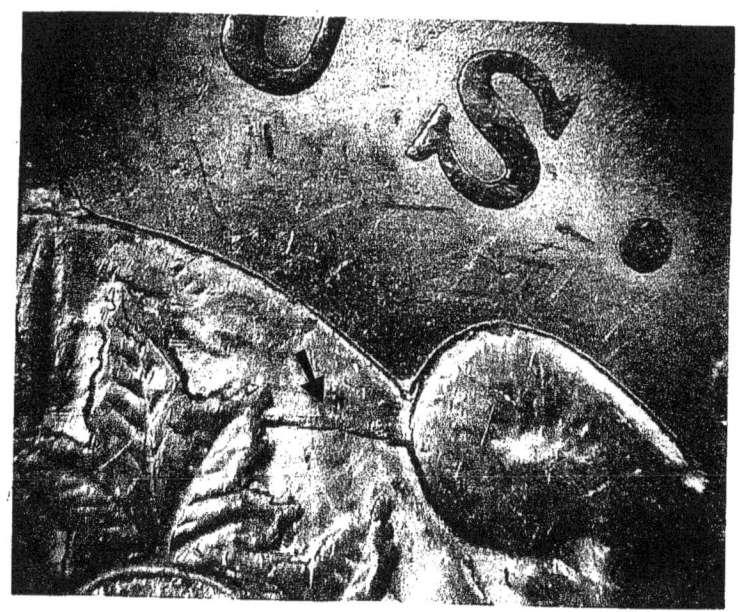

VAM 1B1 Die Gouge in Cap

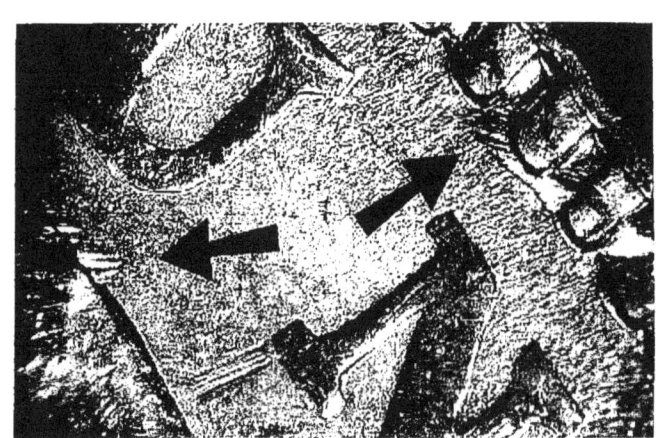

VAM 1B1 Die Gouges Cap Back & Above N

VAM 1B1 Die Gouge Cap Back

VAM 1B2 Die Gouge in Cap

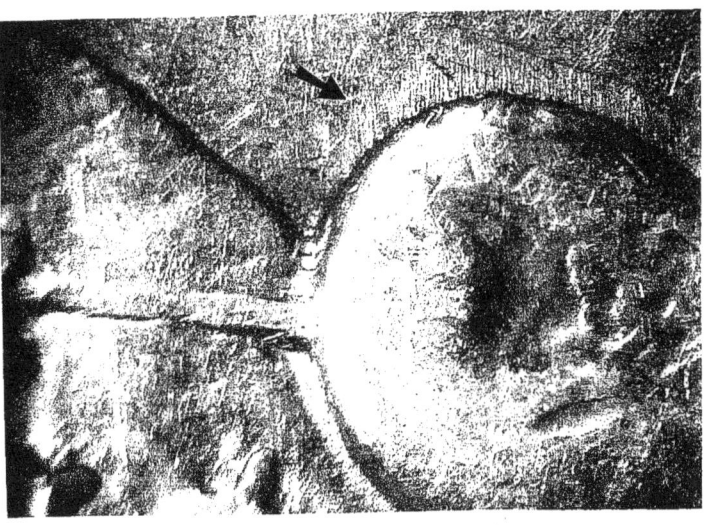

VAM 1B2 Cap Gouge & Polishing Lines

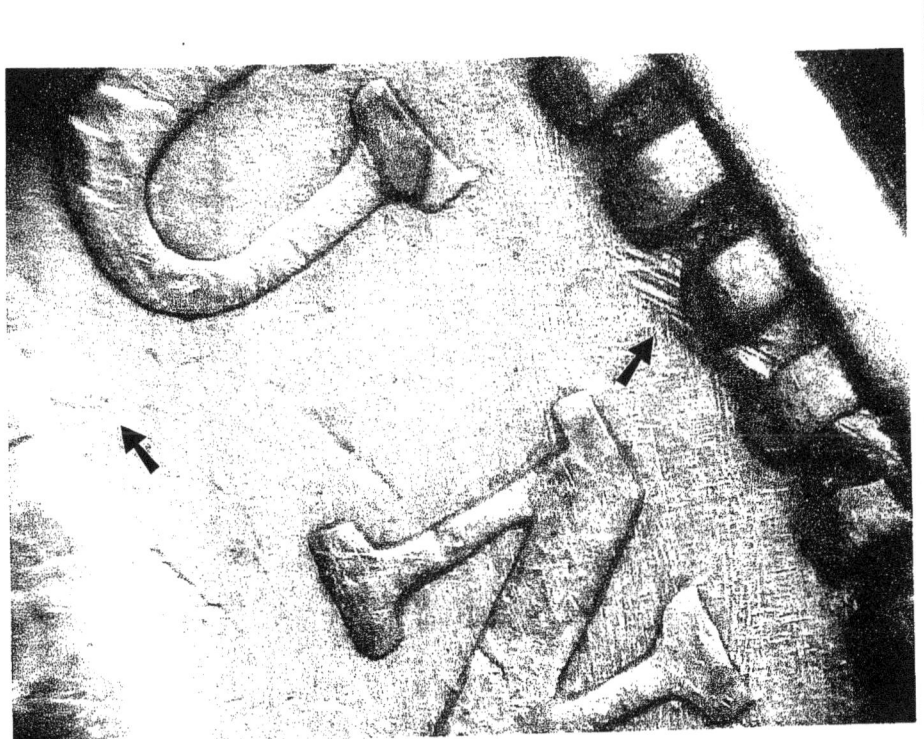

VAM 1B2 Die Gouges Cap Back & Above N

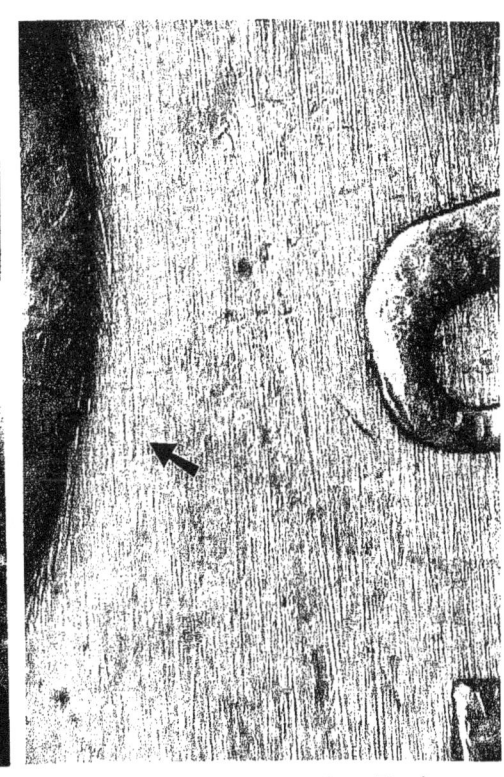

VAM 1B2 Polishing Cap Back

1B3
3rd Die State (Die Damaged)

VAM 1B3 Thorn-Like Die Gouge

VAM 1B3a Polished Cap Back

1B3a
4th Die State (Die Polished)

VAM 1B3a Polished Thorn Die Gouge

VAM 1B3a Die Gouges UN

1B4
5th Die State (Die Damaged)

VAM 1B4 Die Gouge IB

VAM 1B4 Die Gouge NU

1B4a
6th Die State (Die Polished)

VAM 1B4a Polished Die Gouge IB

VAM 1B4a Polished Die Gouge NU

VAM 1B5 Die Gouges IB & Above B

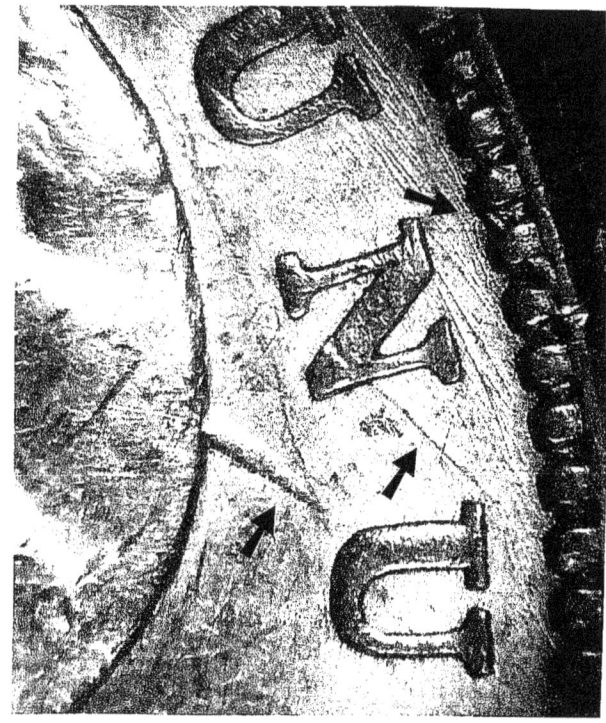

VAM 1B5 Die Gouges NU & Cap

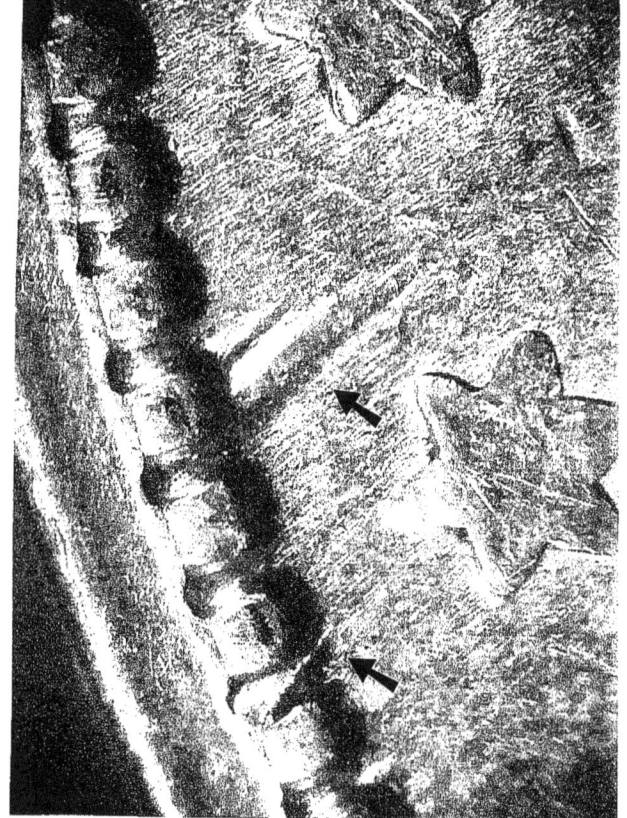

VAM 1B5 Die Gouges 4th Left Star

VAM 1B5 Die Gouge 2nd Rt. Star

VAM 1B6 Polished Die Gouges IB

VAM 1B6 Polished Die Gouges NU

VAM 1B6 Polished Die Gouges 4th Left Star

VAM 1B6 Polished Die Gouge 2nd Rt. Star

VAM 1B7 Die Gouge Y

VAM 1B7 Die Gouge Y & Cap

Die Gouges on Reverse
(With Obverse VAMs 1B5-7)

VAMs 1B5-7 Die Gouge E-D on Reverse

VAMs 1B5-7 Spike Eagle's Left Wing

FURTHER REFERENCES

Please check Amazon Kindle for Michael S. Fey, Ph.D., and Leroy Van Allen & A. George Mallis publications. For hard copy print of books, please contact Dr. Fey at RCI, P.O. Box C, Ironia, NJ 07845 or eMail: Feyms@aol.com.

Hard copy books are also available at *The Institute for Silver Dollar Education and Research*, at website: *Ilovesilver dollars.org* or by contacting Executive Director John Baumgart at John.Baumgart@comcast.net

Amazon Kindle

Fey, Michael S. 2019. *The Complete Virtual Guide to Pricing Your Morgan Silver Dollars*. 286 pp. RCI

Van Allen, Leroy, & A. George Mallis. 2023. *Part I or II or III of Three. Comprehensive Catalog and Encyclopedia or Morgan & Peace Dollars*. RCI Total 520 pp.

Leroy Van Allen. 2011. *Wonders of Morgan Dollars*. 139 pp. RCI

Leroy Van Allen. 2013. *Wonders of Peace Dollars*. 273 pp. RCI

Leroy Van Allen. 2006. *Morgan Dollars 8 & 7 Over 8 Tail Feather Story*. 52 pp. RCI

Leroy Van Allen. 2010. *1878 P 7 Tail Feather Morgan Dollar Attribution Guide*. 130 pp. RCI

Leroy Van Allen. 2006. *1878 S Morgan Dollar Attribution Guide*. 139 pp. RCI

Fey, Michael S. 2009 The Top 100 Morgan Dollar Varieties: The VAM Keys

FURTHER REFERENCES

Hard Copy Books

Fey, Michael S. 2019. The Top 100 Morgan Dollar Varieties: The VAM Keys. 286 pp. RCI

Fey, Michael S. 2008. *A Decade of Top 100 Insights*. RCI 174 pp.

Van Allen, Leroy. 1991. *RotaFlip Die Rotation Booklet and Guide*. 1991. RCI

Kimpton, M.D., Mark. 2005. *Elite Clashed Morgan Dollars*. RCI 160 pp

Van Allen, Leroy, & A. George Mallis. 2023. *Comprehensive Catalog and Encyclopedia or Morgan & Peace Dollars*. RCI Total 520 pp.

Van Allen, Leroy 2011. *Wonders of Morgan Dollars*. 139 pp. RCI

Van Allen, Leroy 2013. *Wonders of Peace Dollars*. 273 pp. RCI

Van Allen, Leroy 2006. *Morgan Dollars 8 & 7 Over 8 Tail Feather Story*. 52 pp. RCI

Van Allen, Leroy 2010. *1878 P 7 Tail Feather Morgan Dollar Attribution Guide*. 130 pp. RCI

Van Allen, Leroy 2006. *1878 S Morgan Dollar Attribution Guide*. 139 pp. RCI

Van Allen, Leroy 2013. *Die Gouges and Scratches Peace Dollar Attribution Guide*. 109 pp RCI

Van Allen, Leroy 2008. *1921 Scribbles Morgan Dollar Attribution Guide*. 234 pp. RCI

Van Allen, Leroy. 2013. *Misplaced Date Digits Morgan Dollar Attribution Guide*. 57 pp RCI

Van Allen, Leroy. 2017. *Dashed Under 8 Morgan Dollar Attribution Guide*. 53 pp. RCI

Van Allen, Leroy. 2009. *Overdates and Over Mint Marks of Morgan Dollar Attribution Guide*. 53 pp. RCI

Van Allen, Leroy. 2015. *Denticle & Die Impressions Morgan Dollar Attribution Guide*. 109 pp. RCI

Van Allen, Leroy. 2009. *1921 P Infrequently Reeded or Wide Reeding Morgan Dollar Attribution Guide*. 31 pp. RCI

Van Allen, Leroy. 2011 *Amazing Changing 1921 S VAM 1B Thorn Head Morgan Dollar*. 2011. 22 pp. RCI

Van Allen, Leroy. 2009. *1889 P Doubled Ear Morgan Dollar Attribution Guide*. 32 pp. RCI

Van Allen, Leroy. 2016. *Micro o and Other Counterfeit Morgan and Peace Dollars*. 191 pp RCI

Van Allen, Leroy. 2005. *Micro o Mint Mark on Morgan Dollars*. 32 pp. RCI

Van Allen, Leroy. 2005. *Die Markers for 1921 Morgan and Peace Proof Dollars*. 9 pp. RCI

Van Allen, Leroy and Baumgart, John. 1992-Date Various VAM Book Yearly Supplements. RCI